TURNING POINTS IN US MILITARY HISTORY

THE ATTACK ON PEARL HARBOR

Charlie Samuels

Gareth Stevens Publishing

Please visit our website, www.garethstevens.com. For a free color catalog of all our high-quality books, call toll-free 1-800-542-2595 or fax 1-877-542-2596.

Library of Congress Cataloging-in-Publication Data

Samuels, Charlie.
The attack on Pearl Harbor / by Charlie Samuels.
 p. cm. — (Turning points in US military history)
Includes index.
ISBN 978-1-4824-0411-1 (pbk.)
ISBN 978-1-4824-3312-8 (6-pack)
ISBN 978-1-4824-0409-8 (library binding)
1. Pearl Harbor (Hawaii), Attack on, 1941 — Juvenile literature. 2. World War, 1939-1945 — Juvenile literature. I. Samuels, Charlie, 1961-. II. Title.
D767.92 S26 2014
940.54—dc23

Published in 2014 by
Gareth Stevens Publishing
111 East 14th Street, Suite 349
New York, NY 10003

© 2014 Brown Bear Books Ltd

For Brown Bear Books Ltd:
Editorial Director: Lindsey Lowe
Managing Editor: Tim Cooke
Children's Publisher: Anne O'Daly
Design Manager: Keith Davis
Designer: Lynne Lennon
Picture Manager: Sophie Mortimer
Production Director: Alastair Gourlay

Picture Credits:
Front Cover: Robert Hunt Library

All images Robert Hunt Library except:
Getty Images: Peter Stackpole/Time & Life Pictures US 19; **US National Archives:** 27, 34, 35, 38, 39, 41; **US Navy:** 17, 18.

All Artworks © Brown Bear Books Ltd

Brown Bear Books has made every attempt to contact the copyright holder. If you have any information please contact smortimer@brownbearbooks.co.uk

Manufactured in the United States of America

CPSIA compliance information: Batch #CW14GS. For further information contact Gareth Stevens, New York, New York at 1-800-542-2595.

CONTENTS

INTRODUCTION

To many Americans, the Japanese air attack on the US Pacific Fleet at Pearl Harbor in Hawaii on December 7, 1941, was a humiliating shock. They were used to believing that the Japanese could not challenge US military power in the Pacific. That view was also shared by many US politicians and military commanders. Pearl Harbor showed how mistaken they were.

A Dangerous Gamble

The Japanese risked everything on destroying the US fleet. They thought this would allow them to build up an empire in Southeast Asia before the United States could recover. They hoped the Americans would then let them keep the empire, rather than fight. When the attack on Pearl Harbor failed to destroy the US fleet, the Japanese gamble ended in disaster.

War on Two Fronts

Before the raid on Pearl Harbor, many Americans had been reluctant to become involved in the war already raging in Europe. The raid changed everything. The next day, Americans enthusiastically supported the US declaration of war on Japan. A few days later, Germany and Italy, allies of Japan, declared war on the United States. Suddenly US forces found themselves facing the prospect of having to fight in both the Pacific and in Europe.

A Japanese pilot took this photograph of burning US battleships in Pearl Harbor during the attack.

Japanese fighters and dive-bombers are prepared for the attack on Pearl Harbor on the flight deck of the aircraft carrier *Akagi*.

Politics in the Pacific

The Japanese attack at Pearl Harbor seemed to come out of the blue. But, in fact the United States and Japan had been rivals in the Pacific since the start of the 20th century. As Japan tried to expand its world influence, it became likely that the two powers would eventually clash.

Japanese troops arrive in China in the 1930s. Japan had invaded Manchuria, in northern China, in September 1931.

Japanese troops take part in the assault on the Chinese city of Wuhan in 1938; the attack was one of the largest battles in history.

Japan had a large population crowded into its relatively small islands. It lacked many natural resources, which had to be imported. These included vital materials such as iron, rubber, and oil. Eighty percent of these imports came by sea via the United States. Japan had built a strong navy to guard its supply lanes.

Imperial Ambition

Japan's ambition to become a major power in the region had grown in the early 20th century. Japan's navy had defeated the Russian fleet at the Battle of Tsushima in 1905. In 1910 it occupied neighboring Korea.

WASHINGTON TREATY

In 1922 the victorious powers in World War I signed a treaty in Washington, DC, restricting the size of their navies. The United States and Britain were allowed 525,000 tons (533,000 t) of shipping, Japan 315,000 (320,000 t), and Italy and France somewhat less. The five nations also agreed not to build more bases in the Pacific. Many Japanese saw the treaty as unfair. It meant plans for a large Japanese fleet had to be cut, and left the United States as the major naval power in the Pacific.

As one of the victors in World War I (1914–1918), Japan took over former German colonies in the Pacific. It used the islands to build military bases.

Growing Pressure

In 1924 both the United States and Australia banned Japanese migration. This added to population pressure within Japan. In the meantime, society within Japan became highly militarized. The army dominated all aspects of life and government.

In 1931 the Japanese army occupied the Chinese province of Manchuria. In 1937 Japan invaded the rest of China. Japanese expansion alarmed the United States, which put limits on Japanese trade. The Japanese,

Japanese troops invade Manchuria in 1931. The army's invasion forced the Japanese government to take over the region.

however, now targeted European colonies in East Asia. In 1940 Japanese troops moved into French-controlled Indochina (modern Vietnam) and threatened the Dutch East Indies. In response, the United States expanded its navy.

A Fateful Decision

The Japanese expanded deeper into Indochina in 1941. The United States limited trade and oil exports to Japan still further. Japan now had only one year of oil reserves remaining. Oil was vital for its army and, especially, its navy. It would either have to stop its expansion plans or fight. It decided to fight.

The US Pacific Fleet at anchor: the Treaty of Washington meant that the US Navy had the largest fleet in the Pacific.

THE PACIFIC FLEET

In May 1940, as tension grew in the Pacific, the US Battle Fleet was moved from California to Pearl Harbor on the island of Oahu, Hawaii. The base was closer to Japan, and the fleet's commander, Admiral James O. Richardson, feared it would be vulnerable to attack. In February 1941, Richardson was replaced by Admiral Husband Kimmel, and the fleet was renamed the Pacific Fleet. The fleet had 3 aircraft carriers, 9 battleships, 12 cruisers, 8 light cruisers, and 50 destroyers.

The War in Europe

German stormtroopers with bicycles pass a group of officers during the invasion of France in May 1940.

War in Europe had been brewing during the 1930s as Adolf Hitler's Germany sought to expand. On September 1, 1939, the Germans invaded Poland. Two days later, Britain and France declared war on Germany. The United States declared itself neutral, but could not avoid involvement in the European war.

Royal Air Force (RAF) pilots rush to their fighters during the Battle of Britain, fought from July to October 1940.

By June 1940, the German army's *Blitzkrieg* (lightning war) had captured France, Norway, Denmark, Belgium, Luxembourg, and the Netherlands. Only Britain remained unoccupied.

New Targets

The Germans prepared for an invasion, but, in the summer of 1940, the British Royal Air Force fought off the German air force in the Battle of Britain. The Germans found new targets. By October, Germany, Italy, and Japan had joined forces. Soon Germany took Romania, and Italy invaded Greece. In April 1941, Germany captured Greece and Yugoslavia. That June three million German troops invaded the Soviet Union in an operation that the Germans codenamed Barbarossa.

FDR AND THE WAR

US President Franklin D. Roosevelt was determined to help Britain fight the Nazis. But many Americans did not want to be involved in what they saw as a European conflict. In 1941 Roosevelt started to supply Britain with weapons under the Lend–Lease Act, which allowed the British to pay for the supplies after the war. But Roosevelt could not send any troops. The attack on Pearl Harbor finally allowed him to declare the war that he had wanted for some time.

The Japanese Plans

Since January 1941, Admiral Isoroku Yamamoto, commander of the Japanese navy, had planned a surprise attack against the US Pacific Fleet. The plan was to land a knock-out blow that would remove the US naval advantage in the Pacific. That would leave the way open for Japan to capture enough territory and resources to wage war until the United States surrendered.

The Japanese battleship *Yamato*, launched a week after the attack on Pearl Harbor, was the largest warship in the world.

Yamamoto believed the Japanese needed to make quick gains in the Pacific before the United States could strike back.

Six carriers were to sail secretly from Japan. They would launch large waves of aircraft to bomb US airfields and destroy the US fighter defenses. Japanese planes would then attack the US Pacific Fleet anchored at Pearl Harbor. The main targets were the US aircraft carriers and the large warships moored along "Battleship Row."

Special Training

Pearl Harbor was only 40 feet (12.2 m) deep. The Japanese used torpedo bombs that powered through the water into their targets. They had to develop special bombs for the shallow harbor. The pilots trained specially at a harbor in Japan.

ADMIRAL YAMAMOTO

Admiral Yamamoto had studied in the United States as a young man, and his time there made him doubt that Japan could win a Pacific war. The United States had too big an advantage in resources and industry. Yamamoto therefore came up with a plan to cripple the US fleet. He based his plan on the successful British air attack on the Italian fleet at Taranto in 1940. Yamamoto devised special torpedoes and armor-piercing bombs for use at Pearl Harbor.

The Fleet Sets Sail

Japanese airmen receive a final briefing about the Pearl Harbor raid shortly before taking off from their carrier.

The Japanese set the Pearl Harbor attack for December 7, 1941. It was a Sunday, so the base personnel would be off guard. On November 26, the Japanese fleet set out on the 4,000-mile (6,400 km) voyage. Diplomatic talks were still going on as the ships neared Hawaii.

The First Air Fleet comprised six aircraft carriers, two battleships, two cruisers, and escort ships. It sailed from the Kurile Islands, north of Japan. Yamamoto took care to make sure it was not detected. It took a long route and sailed in radio silence. No trash was thrown overboard in case it gave away the fleet's presence.

Getting Closer

Submarines sailed ahead of the fleet and dropped midget submarines, which were off Oahu early on December 6. By dawn next day, the fleet was within 200 miles (320 km) of the island. The attack was ready to begin.

DIPLOMATIC COUNTDOWN

As the fleet sailed, the Japanese pretended to negotiate with the United States. Japan's diplomats in Washington were meant to deliver a note effectively declaring war. It should have been delivered just before the attack but delays in translating it meant it was only delivered when Pearl Harbor was under fire.

The Japanese aircraft took off from six aircraft carriers including the *Zuiho*, seen here under fire later in the war.

Pearl Harbor

The Japanese destination was the US naval base at Pearl Harbor on Oahu in Hawaii. From here the US Pacific Fleet could guard the approaches to US territory in the Philippines and the Panama Canal. The base was about 4,000 miles (6,400 km) from Japan. Most US military commanders believed this was too far for it to be a target.

An aerial view of Pearl Harbor before the attack shows how close together ships were moored in the anchorage.

Admiral Husband Kimmel, commander in chief of the US Pacific Fleet, was blamed for not defending the base better against attack.

Pearl Harbor itself was thought to be secure. Antisubmarine patrols and nets protected the entrance from the possibility that a submarine might enter undetected. The harbor was only around 40 feet (12.2 m) deep, which was thought to be too shallow for the Japanese to drop torpedoes from airplanes. Any torpedoes would hit the sea floor.

The Fleet at Anchor

The nearly 100 ships of the Pacific Fleet were berthed around the harbor. The most powerful battleships were lined up on Battleship Row. Some were berthed side-by-side, so that if

BASE COMMANDERS

The two men in charge of Pearl Harbor were criticized after the attack. Admiral Husband Kimmel, commander of the Pacific Fleet, failed to organize air patrols and allowed his fleet to rest at anchor, unprepared for an attack. Land defense was the responsibility of Lieutenant General Walter C. Short. His chief concern was Japanese-American sabotage. He ordered the airplanes to be gathered together to guard against sabotage, ignoring the fact it made them easy targets for air attack.

Walter C. Short ordered airplanes to be parked together for defense against sabotage; in fact, it made them an easier target for aerial bombing.

a torpedo was ever fired from a submarine or airplane that had gotten into the harbor, it would not be able to reach the ships on the inside.

Air Support

To protect the fleet when it was in the anchorage, there were hundreds of airplanes based at Army and Navy airfields across Oahu. As many as 3,000 antiaircraft and naval guns were also positioned to protect the bases and the islands. Forty-three thousand US Army and Air Corps troops were stationed at barracks around the island, ready to fight off any amphibious landings.

Fighting at Long Range

Among Pearl Harbor's other defenses were radar and patrol planes. Their job was to detect any enemy approach to the islands while it was still far out at sea and then to intercept the enemy while it was at such a long range as to be harmless. No wonder the US Army Chief of Staff, General George Marshall, called Pearl Harbor the "strongest fortress in the world."

The Wrong Enemy

The commander at Pearl Harbor was General Walter Short. He was less worried about a Japanese attack than he was about sabotage by Japanese Americans living in Hawaii. A few Japanese Americans had, in fact, spied on the US fleet for Japan. Despite all the defenses on Hawaii, however, the failure to use them effectively meant the Japanese attack on the fleet took place almost unopposed.

An American soldier uses mounted binoculars to watch the skies for any sign of enemy aircraft.

US DEFENSES

The US defenses on Oahu had many weaknesses. The harbor was thought too shallow for torpedo attacks, so torpedo nets were not used to protect the ships. The Army's modern radar was only used for a few hours each day. The aircraft on the island were not ready for immediate use. Air patrols were not as frequent as they should have been. There was also a lack of coordination between the two commanders, Kimmel and Short.

The First Wave

A long-range Zero fighter prepares to take off from a Japanese carrier as part of the first wave heading toward Pearl Harbor.

The first wave of the Japanese attack on Pearl Harbor consisted of 183 airplanes. The attack began at 7:48 A.M. on Sunday morning, December 7, and lasted just 15 minutes. In that time, Oahu's airfields were hit and most of the airplanes were destroyed on the ground. This made sure there would be no US air defense against the second wave.

In the early hours of December 7, 1941, the five midget submarines off the coast of Oahu got ready to enter Pearl Harbor. One of the vessels tried to slip into the harbor as the anti-submarine net was opened. It was spotted and US ships fired on it at 6:30 A.M. The incident was not reported immediately, however, so neither naval or army commanders knew about it.

Takeoff at Sea

At the same time, some 200 miles (320 km) away, the Japanese First Air Fleet got ready to launch its planes from the six aircraft carriers. The pilots were buoyed by the sight of the rising sun that reminded them of their national flag.

ACHIEVING SECRECY

To achieve the surprise attack the Japanese Fleet had succeeded in sailing 4,000 miles (6,400 km) across the Pacific Ocean without being detected. All the vessels maintained radio silence, so that US intelligence would not be able to track the fleet's route. In fact, the unusual lack of any kind of Japanese radio traffic in the Pacific did arouse the suspicions of US intelligence—but they did not act on it. The United States had managed to overlook what could have been a vital clue as to Japan's intentions.

Plumes of water rise from explosions as a Japanese aircraft flies over Pearl Harbor in this photo taken from another Japanese plane.

At Pearl Harbor, US radar operators saw what appeared to be a large mass of planes approaching on their screens. When they reported them, they were told it was a flight of US B-17 bombers that were expected from the mainland.

Air Attack

Shortly afterward, some 54 dive-bombers then attacked Wheeler Field and Ford Island, and 45 Zero fighters attacked the other airfields. The pilots targeted airstrips, hangars, workshops, and parked airplanes. The expected flight of US B-17s arrived in the middle of the attack. Most survived and landed safely. Meantime, 90 bombers attacked the Pacific Fleet with bombs and torpedoes.

A rescue boat approaches the burning hull of USS *West Virginia* after it had been hit by a number of torpedoes and bombs.

Five Type A midget submarines took part in the attack; this one was deliberately beached by its crew on Oahu.

The US aircraft carriers were out at sea, so the Japanese targeted the seven battleships along Battleship Row (an eighth was nearby in dry dock). As US naval personnel rushed to their stations, the USS *Oklahoma* and *West Virginia* were torpedoed. The USS *Arizona* blew up.

Radio Signals

The attack had taken just 15 minutes. The Japanese pilots sent the victory signal, "Tora! Tora! Tora!" That meant they had achieved complete surprise. On the US side, Admiral Kimmel also sent a signal to the rest of the US fleet: "Air raid on Pearl Harbor. This is not drill."

MIDGET SUBMARINES

The Japanese Type A Ko-hyoteki midget submarines were strapped to larger submarines for the long journey to Pearl Harbor. They were released close to the destination. The midget craft had two crew and conditions on board cramped. Each but non actu fire the be ti

23

The Second Wave

The second wave of Japanese fighters, bombers, and dive-bombers took off about 40 minutes after the first wave had left the carriers. The attacks had to be split because the raid involved so many Japanese airplanes that it was not possible to launch them all at the same time.

Casualties burn on Battleship Row: USS *West Virginia* (left), USS *Tennessee* (center), and USS *Arizona* (right).

The superior performance of the Zero gave Japanese pilots a decisive advantage in the early years of the Pacific war.

This time, 176 aircraft swept around the east coast of Oahu. Their mission was to attack the same targets as the first wave and destroy any ships, airplanes, and facilities that had managed to survive.

US Air Defenses

The island was now on full alert. A handful of Army fighter aircraft managed to take off from Wheeler Field and, even though they were massively outnumbered, they still shot down 11 Japanese planes. However, no US Navy aircraft made it into the air during either of the Japanese attacks.

MITSUBISHI ZERO

The Japanese Mitsubishi A6M Zero played a key role in the attacks on Pearl Harbor. The long-range fighter plane was designed to take off from aircraft carriers. Although it was primarily a fighter plane, it could also carry bombs, as it did at Pearl Harbor. In the early part of the war, the Zero had a far superior performance to any US fighter. By mid-1942, however, a combination of new tactics and better equipment enabled US pilots to engage the Zero on more equal terms.

The destroyer USS *Shaw* explodes after bombs strike its forward magazine; the ship was repaired within a few months of the attack.

Thanks to the Army fighters and the antiaircraft fire that filled the sky, a total of 20 Japanese planes were shot down compared to eight in the first wave.

Escape of the *Nevada*

The battleship *Nevada*, on Battleship Row, had already been hit earlier but successfully shot down several planes. With the nearby *Arizona* on fire, the *Nevada* risked catching fire, too. The ship's captain tried to sail away from danger, but that attracted the firepower of the second wave of Japanese planes. The captain realized that if the ship sank in the harbor's channel, it would be blocked for months. To avoid this, he steered the *Nevada* to beach it out of the way.

Many of the battleships were on fire or sinking. The Japanese planes now concentrated on the northern part of the harbor, but they failed to hit the berthed cruisers or oil-storage tanks they targeted.

Heading for Home

The Japanese pilots wanted to launch a third wave of attacks. Admiral Nagumo decided against this. He was concerned that the US carriers at sea might come after his fleet. The attack was over.

DORRIE MILLER

Doris "Dorrie" Miller was a cook in the US Navy. He was on duty on the USS *West Virginia* when the alarm sounded. He headed for the deck, where he carried wounded sailors to safety. Then he fired a machine gun at enemy planes until he ran out of ammunition. For his bravery, he became the first African American to be awarded the Navy Cross.

As an African American, Dorrie Miller was only supposed to perform supporting duties rather than front-line fighting.

Death of the Arizona

The *Arizona* leans heavily to the side after the explosion that caused it to sink. Hundreds of sailors were trapped below deck.

On December 6, 1941, the battleship USS *Arizona* was tied up next to a repair ship at Pearl Harbor. It was loaded with almost 1.5 million gallons of fuel in preparation for a trip to the mainland later in the month. The next day, Japanese bombers targeted the ship.

At the start of the attack, the battleship was hit four times by bombs. Few of the crew even had the chance to get to their battle stations. The ship's commanding officers were both killed on the bridge.

Fatal Explosion

Ten minutes later, a bomb penetrated the forward magazine, setting off tons of explosives. The force of the blast lifted the *Arizona* into the air, then it sank in the shallow water. The wreck burned for two days. Almost half of the day's 2,400 deaths—1,177 sailors—died on the *Arizona*. Today the wreck remains as a memorial.

The superstructure of the *Arizona* is visible above the shallow waters of Pearl Harbor in the aftermath of the attack.

EYEWITNESS

"It seemed as though the magazines forward blew up while we were hooking up the fire hose, as the noise was followed by an awful 'swish' and hot air blew out of the compartments. There had been bomb hits at the first start, and yellowish smoke was pouring out of the hatches from below deck. There were lots of men coming out on the quarterdeck with every stitch of clothing and shoes blown off, painfully burned and shocked."

Donald A. Graham, Aviation Machinist's Mate, USS *Arizona*

The Airfields

As US ships burned in Pearl Harbor, all over Oahu hundreds of US aircraft were destroyed while they were on the ground. The Japanese targeted the four US Army airfields, the naval air stations at Ford Island and Kaneohe Bay, and the Marine air station at Ewa.

Sailors fight fires among the aircraft at Ford Naval Station: 33 of the base's 70 aircraft were destroyed in the attack.

Smoke billows from Wheeler Army Airfield; some 15 pilots managed to get into the air from the base and fought with Japanese aircraft.

The Japanese pilots flew over deserted airfields. The US planes were lined up close together in neat rows as a precaution against sabotage. The fighters machine-gunned the planes and the dive-bombers dropped their bombs on aircraft and hangars. There was no real opposition.

A Weak Response

On the ground, US crews rushed to get the few planes that were serviceable into the air. Most of the planes were unarmed, however, so they were not ready for immediate combat. The ground crews worked furiously as the bombs fell around them. Many pilots were killed as they tried to get their planes airborne. Only a handful made it into the air to challenge the attackers.

CASUALTIES OF THE JAPANESE RAID

A total of 2,403 US servicemen died at Pearl Harbor, and 1,178 were wounded. The Navy accounted for 2,008 of the dead, with the single largest loss of life on board the USS *Arizona*. Of the 301 US airplanes on Oahu, only 52 were left fit to use. All eight US battleships were damaged; four were sunk or capsized, although all but two were later repaired. The Japanese lost 29 planes, five midget submarines, and one submarine, plus 64 pilots and sailors.

THE ATTACK ON PEARL HARBOR

Aftermath at Pearl Harbor

The Japanese attack left the US base in ruins—along with US naval power in the Pacific. Along with the loss of life, many ships of the Pacific Fleet and nearly all its airplanes had been destroyed. The outrage that greeted news of the attack transformed the United States.

The USS *Cassin* and USS *Downes* were badly damaged during the raid, but new ships were built around their salvaged equipment.

Japanese soldiers raise the Rising Sun flag during the invasion of the Philippines, which began the day after Pearl Harbor.

While the returning Japanese pilots celebrated, Admiral Yamamoto did not. He knew the victory was only temporary. The United States was bound to strike back. He was right. The US Pacific Fleet was mostly repaired. More importantly, the US carriers were undamaged. They would be vital to future US success.

A United Nation

The sneak attack had humiliated the United States. But it united the nation behind avenging the attack. Yamamoto was right: the "victory" at Pearl Harbor would prove to be a strategic and tactical disaster.

JAPAN'S ASIAN ADVANCE

Within hours of the attack on Pearl Harbor, Japan launched assaults across Southeast Asia. With the US Pacific Fleet out of action, the Japanese swept through Guam, Wake Island, Burma, Malaya, Singapore, Hong Kong, and the Philippines. They enjoyed rapid successes against US, British, and Dutch defenders. In the Philippines, General Douglas MacArthur's US troops proved as ill-prepared as the defenders had been at Pearl Harbor.

Reaction in the United States

This poster for the US Navy appeals to the anger many Americans felt about what they saw as a sneaky and cowardly attack.

News of the Japanese attack on Pearl Harbor stunned Americans. Many people feared a Japanese attack on the mainland. The country was on high alert. On the West Coast, sirens blared out to warn of an invasion after Japanese aircraft carriers were reported offshore. But the reports turned out to be mistaken.

Civilian volunteers taking part in a first-aid drill in Washington, DC, transfer a "casualty" to the hospital in a taxi cab.

A black out was introduced in Los Angeles and San Francisco. No lights could be shown at night, so that enemy planes would not be able to see their targets. Troops were sent to guard key buildings and factories. Machine-gun posts were erected around the White House and other government buildings in Washington, DC.

Nervous Times

People were jumpy. Fear of spies and saboteurs led to the harassment of Japanese Americans. Soon thousands of them would be interned. Patriotism surged as men flocked to recruiting stations to join the armed forces.

AIR-RAID PRECAUTIONS

Cities across the United States were blacked out so that Japanese bombers would not be able to see their targets. Radio stations stopped broadcasting so enemy planes would not be able to follow their signal. Air-raid drills were held in which sirens warned people to take cover in shelters. Civilian Defense organized 10 million volunteers to act as firefighters and first-aiders in case of attack. In the event, however, no enemy bombers reached the mainland during the war.

The United States Enters the War

President Franklin D. Roosevelt calls on the US Congress to declare war on Japan, on December 8, 1941.

Within hours of the attack at Pearl Harbor, political leaders in Washington, DC, were lining up to support a declaration of war. Even politicians who had wanted to stay out of the war in Europe now called for war with Japan.

The day after the raid, Monday, December 8, President Roosevelt addressed a joint session of Congress. He asked for a declaration of war on Japan. All but one Representative agreed. That afternoon, Roosevelt signed the declaration.

War in Europe

On December 11, Japan's allies, Germany and Italy, declared war on the United States. Congress voted unanimously to declare war on the Axis powers. The United States was now firmly at war in Europe and the Pacific.

THE DAY OF INFAMY

Roosevelt's address to Congress on December 8 was broadcast live on the radio. In one of the most famous of all presidential addresses, he gave Pearl Harbor the name by which it is often known: "Yesterday, December 7, 1941—a day which will live in infamy—the United States of America was suddenly and deliberately attacked by naval and air forces of the Empire of Japan."

Roosevelt signs the formal declaration of war on Japan on December 8; three days later, the United States was also at war in Europe.

Japanese Internment

In the weeks after Pearl Harbor, many people feared that Japanese-Americans would spy for the Japanese or carry out sabotage against the United States. They called for people of Japanese descent to be moved away from the Pacific coastal region, so that they would not be able to help any attempted Japanese invasion.

A Japanese-American storekeeper displays a sign to try to prevent losing any business to people who might suspect his loyalty.

Watched by soldiers, Japanese-Americans wait at Santa Anita Assembly Center to be sent to relocation camps.

In February 1942 President Roosevelt issued Executive Order 9066, which allowed anywhere in the United States to be declared a military zone. The order was used to remove people of Japanese origin from all of California and much of Oregon, Washington, and Arizona.

Losing Their Rights

Of the 127,000 people of Japanese origin in the United States, almost 120,000 were forced to move to so-called relocation centers. Some 80,000 were US citizens. The detainees lost their homes and businesses. They were unable to leave the camps and were guarded by armed troops and barbed wire. The camps were finally closed in January 1945 when the detainees were allowed to return home.

JAPANESE SERVICEMEN

Once the United States joined the war, the US military discharged all servicemen of Japanese origin. As the conflict went on, however, some 33,000 Japanese-Americans volunteered for the military, including many detainees from the camps. They generally served in Europe, but some volunteers served in the Pacific campaign as special forces. Some 6,000 Japanese Americans also worked for US intelligence, translating Japanese messages.

Who Was to Blame?

Immediately after Pearl Harbor, Americans wanted to know how the most devastating attack ever on the United States was allowed to happen. People still wonder today. Over the decades, eight inquiries have been held to try to discover the answer.

President Roosevelt chats with British prime minister Winston Churchill. Some people believe he wanted an excuse to enter the war on Britain's side.

Immediately after the attack, Admiral Kimmel and General Short were charged with not having adequately prepared the defenses on Oahu. In 1999 the US Senate finally voted 52–47 to clear them of the blame.

A False Sense of Security

In reality the fault lay with US political and military leaders. Many chose not to believe the clear signs that Japan was preparing for an attack. They did not think that the Japanese had the military capability to launch an attack from so far away. US commanders also wrongly believed that they had turned Oahu into an impregnable fortress.

CONSPIRACY THEORIES

A popular conspiracy theory about Pearl Harbor is that President Roosevelt knew about the attack. He allowed it to happen because he wanted to find a way to get the United States into the war. However, there is no proof Roosevelt knew what was about to happen. Although some people suspected that a Japanese attack might be imminent, it could have come anywhere in the Pacific, not necessarily at Pearl Harbor.

Japanese diplomats visit Secretary of State Cordell Hull just before Pearl Harbor. Even they were kept in the dark about the coming raid.

Pearl Harbor to Midway

The *Enterprise*, like the other US carriers, escaped the attack at Pearl Harbor. They became the foundation of US policy in the Pacific.

By the end of April 1942, just five months after the attack on Pearl Harbor, Japan controlled much of the southwest Pacific and Southeast Asia. However, as Admiral Yamamoto had predicted, the victory at Pearl Harbor only brought the Japanese a temporary advantage. The United States recovered from the raid and began an unstoppable advance across the Pacific.

Douglas Devastators are shown on a carrier deck. While Japan lost irreplaceable aircraft and pilots, the United States was able to replace its losses.

The rapid US recovery was possible because the Japanese had failed to destroy the US aircraft carriers at Pearl Harbor. The damage to the fleet was also quickly repaired. The carriers would act as floating bases for US air power.

First Steps to Victory

In April 1942, a small force of US carrier-launched aircraft bombed Japan for the first time. The next month, the US fleet pushed back the Japanese at the Battle of the Coral Sea. A month later, the Japanese tried to seize Midway Island to lure US carriers into battle. But US intelligence had deciphered the naval code and US carrier aircraft sank four Japanese carriers. The Americans lost just one carrier.

VICTORY IN THE PACIFIC

The Japanese failure to destroy the US carriers at Pearl Harbor ultimately cost them dearly. The victory the US carriers won at Midway in June 1942 was a turning point in the war. It ended the Japanese advance in the Pacific. Now US forces began to fight their way from island to island across the ocean to get within range of Japan. In August 1945, Japan surrendered after US planes dropped atomic bombs on the cities of Hiroshima and Nagasaki.

TIMELINE

1931 Japan invades the mineral-rich northern Chinese province of Manchuria.

1937 Japan invades China and begins a brutal campaign of conquest; most of China is in Japanese hands by the end of 1938.

1939 September 1: War breaks out in Europe with Germany's invasion of Poland.

1940 July 22: Prince Konoye becomes prime minister of Japan and introduces a hardline militarism.
September 27: Japan joins the Tripartite Pact with Germany and Italy.
September: Japanese forces invade northern French Indochina (Vietnam).

1941 July: Japanese forces invade southern Indochina; in retaliation, Americans, British, and Dutch place a trade embargo on Japan.
November 5: The Japanese government decides to go to war if the US oil embargo is not relaxed.
November 26: US Secretary of State Cordell Hull demands that Japan withdraw from China, Manchuria, and Indochina. On the same day, the Japanese Combined Fleet sets sail for Pearl Harbor.
December 6: President Franklin D. Roosevelt authorizes the secret Manhattan Project to develop the nuclear bomb.
December 7: The Japanese First Air Fleet launches a massive air assault on the US Pacific Fleet at Pearl Harbor.
December 8: President Roosevelt asks Congress to declare war on Japan. The Japanese launch offensives throughout the Pacific in Malaya, Burma, and the Philippines; they also attack the US base on Wake Island.

December 22: Roosevelt and the British prime minister, Winston Churchill, agree to defeat Germany before turning to Japan.

1942   February 19: Japanese–Americans are moved from the Pacific Coast to relocation centers.
April 9: US forces surrender in the Philippines.
April 18: In the Doolittle Raid, 16 carrier-based US B-25s bomb Japan for the first time.
May 4–6: The Battle of the Coral Sea halts Japanese expansion in the Pacific.
June 3–5: US carriers win a decisive victory at the Battle of Midway.

1943   February: After months of fighting, US forces capture Guadalcanal.
November: US forces land in the Gilbert and Marshall Islands.

1944   June 15: US forces land in the Mariana Islands.
June 20: Japan loses most of its remaining naval strength in the Battle of the Philippine Sea.
October 24: The Japanese navy suffers a final defeat in the Battle of Leyte Gulf.

1945   March 16: US Marines complete the capture of Iwo Jima, only 700 miles (1,125 km) from Japan.
April 1: US forces land on Okinawa.
May: US bomber raids devastate Tokyo.
August 6: An atomic bomb devastates Hiroshima.
August 8: A second atomic bomb is dropped on Nagasaki.
August 15: Emperor Hirohito tells the Japanese people that he has decided to surrender; all Japanese forces will surrender by the end of the month.

GLOSSARY

amphibious An attack in which attackers land from the sea.

barracks Buildings used to house military personnel.

battleship The largest type of warship, with powerful guns and strong armor.

battle stations The positions a ship's crew take up if an attack is imminent.

berth A space for a ship to dock or drop anchor; also, the act of dropping anchor.

colony An overseas territory controlled by a distant country.

conspiracy theory An explanation of an event that suggests some kind of secret intention behind it.

diplomat Someone who represents a government in international affairs.

dive-bomber An airplane that approaches in a near-vertical dive to drop its bombs.

hangar A shelter where aircraft are stored.

internment The confinement of enemy citizens during wartime, usually without any trial.

magazine A storeroom on a warship where ammunition is kept.

neutral Not taking part in or supporting either side in a war or dispute.

radar A system that uses radio waves to detect remote objects.

sabotage Destroying equipment and transportation networks to disrupt enemy operations.

torpedo A missile launched from a plane or ship that uses a small motor to travel underwater to its target.

torpedo net An underwater barrier designed to protect targets from torpedoes.

FURTHER INFORMATION

Books

Dougherty, Steve. *Pearl Harbor: The US Enters World War II* (24/7 Goes to War). Scholastic Library Publishing, 2009.

Lassieur, Allison. *The Attack on Pearl Harbor: An Interactive History Adventure* (You Choose Books). Capstone Press, 2008.

Stein, Conrad. *World War II in the Pacific: From Pearl Harbor to Nagasaki* (United States at War). Enslow Publishers, 2011.

Tarshis, Lauren. *I Survived the Bombing of Pearl Harbor 1941* (I Survived). Turtleback, 2011

Wukovits, John. *The Bombing of Pearl Harbor* (World History). Lucent Books, 2011.

Websites

education.nationalgeographic.com/ education/multimedia/ interactive/pearl-harbor/?ar_a=1
National Geographic Education site on "Remembering Pearl Harbor."

www.history.com/topics/pearl-harbor
History.com Pearl Harbor page with many links.

www.eyewitnesstohistory.com/ pearl.htm
Detailed eyewitness account of the sinking of the USS *Arizona*.

www.historyplace.com/ worldwar2/timeline/pearl.htm
The History Place timeline of the war in the Pacific.

Publisher's note to educators and parents: Our editors have carefully reviewed these websites to ensure that they are suitable for students. Many websites change frequently, however, and we cannot guarantee that a site's future contents will continue to meet our high standards of quality and educational value. Be advised that students should be closely supervised whenever they access the Internet.

INDEX